The Cup

Written by Fiona Undrill
Illustrated by Sarah Hoyle

Collins

I tug the cap.

3

I go up top.

I can get it!

I go in mud.

I muck it up.

I sit in mud.

I get up and go.

I am mad and sad.

Meg gets the cup!

I am not sad.

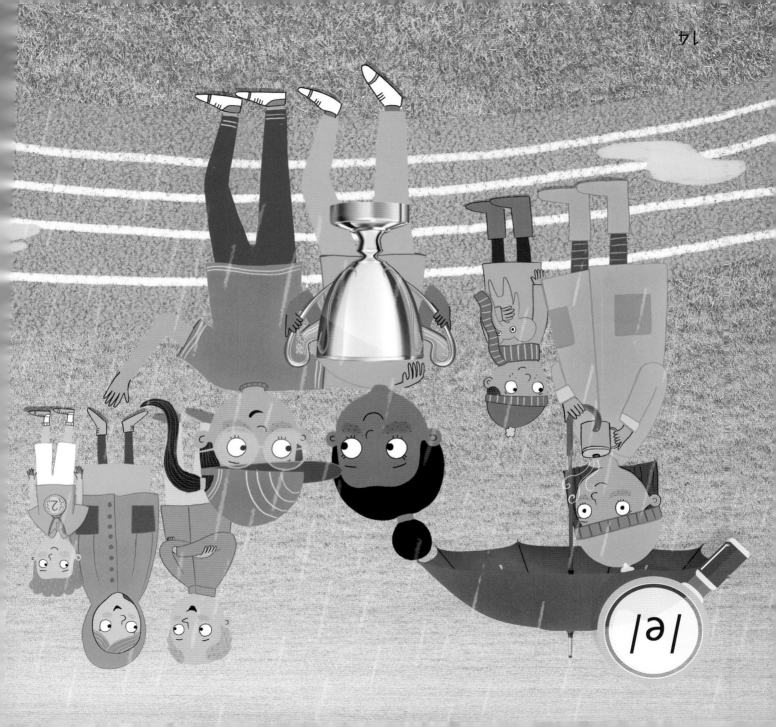

15

Letters and Sounds: Phase 2

Word count: 50

Focus phonemes: /g/ /o/ /c/ /k/ /e/ /u/ ck

Common exception words: I, the, go, and

Curriculum links: Personal, Social and Emotional Development: Managing feelings and behaviour; Making relationships

Early learning goals: Reading: read and understand simple sentences; use phonic knowledge to decode regular words and read them aloud accurately; read some common irregular words; demonstrate understanding when talking with others about what they have read

Developing fluency

- Encourage your child to have fun practising reading the words in the speech bubbles with expression. Can they use different voices or tones?
- Encourage your child to sound talk and then blend the words, e.g. g/e/t **get**, m/u/ck **muck**, c/u/p **cup**. It may help to point to each sound as your child reads.
- Reread the text to your child, modelling fluency and expression.

Phonic practice

- Ask your child to sound talk and blend each of the following words: t/u/g, c/o/p, K/a/t, M/e/g, m/u/ck
- Can your child think of any words that rhyme with **Meg**? (e.g. peg, leg, beg)
- Look at the "I spy sounds" pages (14–15). Discuss the picture with your child. Can they find items/ examples of words containing the /e/ and /u/ sounds? (umbrella, mug, hug, under, elephant, egg, red, Meg, wet, yellow)

Extending vocabulary

- Ask your child:
  - This book is about a **cup**. What other words can we use that mean **cup**? (e.g. trophy, medal, award)
  - On page 11, Kat is feeling **mad**. Can you think of another word for **mad**? (e.g. cross, angry)
  - What other emotions are there? (e.g. happy, sad, scared, excited)